How Moose Learned to Swim

Written by Patrick Lay

Illustrated by Omar Aranda

Flying Start
to Literacy®

T0363475

Contents

Chapter 1:
Looking for food

It was summer in the forest and Moose had plenty to eat. He liked to eat the green leaves and ripe berries that grew in the forest.

But best of all, Moose liked to graze
on the green plants at the lake.

The plants grew all over the lake, but
Moose could only eat the plants at the
edge of the lake, because he could
not swim.

And he ate and ate and ate.

When winter came, snow covered the forest. Food was hard to find.

Every day, Moose looked for food in the forest, but all he could find were twigs and bark.

"I'm sick of eating twigs and bark," said Moose. "I want something nice to eat!"

Then Moose remembered the green plants in the lake.

"I will go to the lake," he said, "and eat the fresh, green water plants."

Chapter 2:
An icy problem

When Moose got to the lake, it was frozen. A thick layer of ice covered the whole lake.

"The plants must be under the water," said Moose. "How will I get to the plants so I can eat them?"

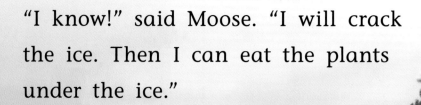

"I know!" said Moose. "I will crack the ice. Then I can eat the plants under the ice."

So Moose stamped on the ice.

Stamp! Stamp! Stamp!
But the ice did not crack.

Moose did not give up.
Every day, he came back to the lake
and stamped on it.

And still the ice did not crack.

Chapter 3:

Danger under the ice

Moose didn't know that catfish lived in the lake under the ice.
And the catfish did not like Moose stamping on the ice!

"Moose is making too much noise," said the leader of the catfish. "When the ice melts, let's scare Moose away. Then he will never bother us again."

"But how?" said the other catfish. "Moose is big and strong and we are small."

"I have a plan," said the leader of the catfish.

When spring arrived, the ice on the lake melted.

"Moose will be here soon to eat the water plants," said the leader of the catfish. "Get your spikes ready."

The catfish hid at the bottom of the lake and waited for Moose.

Chapter 4:

A surprise for Moose

The next time Moose went to the lake, he was happy to see that the ice had melted.

"At last!" he cried. "I can eat the water plants."

Moose stepped into the water and
began to eat the plants. The more
plants Moose ate, the deeper
he went into the lake.

He went deeper and deeper and deeper into the lake.

"Get ready, go!" said the leader of the catfish. And he poked his spike into Moose's leg.

"Ouch!" cried Moose.

Then all the catfish attacked Moose with their spikes.

"Ouch! Ouch! Ouch!" cried Moose.

Moose lifted up his legs to get away from the spikes. He lifted them higher and higher.

Moose was swimming!
He swam and swam and swam.
He kept swimming until he was
safely away from the angry catfish
and their sharp, painful spikes.

Chapter 5:
Some lessons learned

And that is how the very big Moose became such a very good swimmer. And he swam all over the lake to get food.

And catfish are always ready with their spikes . . . just in case!

A note from the author

When I first saw photographs of moose swimming, I was astonished – how could such large animals swim so gracefully?

This got me wondering – when people first saw moose swimming, what did they think? How would they have explained it? And so, the idea of writing a traditional tale to explain this unexpected animal behaviour was born.